BRITAIN IN PICTURES
THE BRITISH PEOPLE IN PICTURES

EARLY BRITAIN

GENERAL EDITOR
W. J. TURNER

The Editor is most grateful to all those who have
so kindly helped in the selection of illustrations
especially to officials of the various public
Museums Libraries and Galleries and
to all others who have generously
allowed pictures and MSS
to be reproduced

EARLY BRITAIN

JACQUETTA HAWKES

WITH
8 PLATES IN COLOUR
AND
26 ILLUSTRATIONS IN
BLACK & WHITE

COLLINS · 14 ST. JAMES'S PLACE · LONDON
MCMXLVI

PRODUCED BY
ADPRINT LIMITED LONDON

FIRST PUBLISHED 1945
SECOND IMPRESSION 1946

PRINTED IN GREAT BRITAIN BY
CLARKE & SHERWELL LTD NORTHAMPTON
ON MELLOTEX BOOK PAPER MADE BY
TULLIS RUSSELL & CO LTD MARKINCH SCOTLAND

LIST OF ILLUSTRATIONS

PLATES IN COLOUR

BLACK AND WHITE ILLUSTRATIONS

THE HUNTERS

SOME years ago when I was taking part in the excavation of an Old Stone Age cave dwelling in the foothills of Mount Carmel, a raw-skinned sandy-haired officer of the Black Watch came out to see our work. It so happened that just at the time of his visit we had laid bare the primitive skeleton of a woman; the skull was low, brow-ridges heavy and the jawbone was chinless, sloping straight back from the teeth. The skeleton sprawled there rather pathetically on the terrace outside the cave, lying among the bones of gazelle and other game which the palæolithic hunters had killed. The officer stared for a long time and grew oppressively silent. He broke the silence only at tea in camp when he suddenly exclaimed, "She must have been up there before Eve then?" I have not forgotten the expression in his eyes as they stared through pale lashes at some terrifying horizon.

It is not surprising that a sudden revelation of this kind overtaking an individual during an afternoon's walk should bring terror. I often think it more remarkable that our species as a whole has taken the news of its biological evolution as calmly as it has, for within the life of the species this is a revelation at least as sudden as the Scotsman's. It is difficult to realise that historians as late as the nineteenth century were writing against a vista which closed, only a few thousand years before the Romans, on the tableau of a divine creation. The brain, whose ancient low-pitched roof was to be seen on Mount Carmel, has played us curious tricks. The more astonishing its achievements grow, the more it has been obliged to humble the self-esteem of its owners. First it made men abandon their comfortable conception of an obsequious universe revolving round their earth then robbed them of their divine creation and told them to look through a microscope at single-celled amoeba with some sense of kinship. The spiritual effect of these profound changes in our background, of these disenchantments presided over by Copernicus and Darwin, are not often analysed, but must be very great.

That they have, however, been assimilated is well shown by the fact that an essay on the half million or so years of human history preceding the Anglo-Saxon invasions should be included in a general series of this kind.

History as it has generally been taught in school encourages a craving for dates : they seem to be necessary to give solidity to reconstructions of the past. Field archæologists know too well that the first question likely to be asked by visitors to their excavations is, "What exactly was the date . . ?" Since the time some six thousand years ago when he began to be a serious agriculturalist man has been obliged to take an exact interest in the seasonal procession, to devise calendars and to record the passage of years. By piecing together his early records and devoting great labour and ingenuity to extending them backward in time and outward in space to regions where no records were kept, prehistorians have gone far towards making it possible to answer questions of date with tolerable accuracy.

Inevitably, however, the accuracy decreases with the increase of antiquity and dates given to anything earlier than the end of the European Ice Age about ten thousand years ago are mere approximations. Nevertheless to meet the persistent question "when" it has become customary to say that the emergence of the human species took place at least half a million years ago. This figure, as overwhelming to the historian as it is trivial to the astronomer, has little more than symbolic significance, yet serves to emphasise that this chapter covers a period at least a hundred times longer than all the others together.

The immense slowness of change implied by such a time scale must be grasped by the imagination before any just conception of this first phase of human development is possible. It is true that the minds of many people are not notably more active or better equipped than they were ten thousand years ago, and that extraordinary mental anomalies persist in our society, but in our material culture we have come to accept continuous rapid development as inevitable. Every year the shapes of motor cars, ships and aeroplanes are changed for greater efficiency and all manner of new discoveries, inventions and gadgets are put before us. Living in the midst of all this, can it be understood that the stone implements which mark the emergence of the earliest men must for them have been more like its hooves to a horse than, say, a pneumatic drill to ourselves. For very many more generations than those separating us from the builders of the pyramids men made the same simple movements to shape the same simple tools which were to serve as natural and unalterable extensions to their hands. The miracle was that development took place at all, and with an acceleration that leads directly to the twentieth century.

A rough picture of some at least among the earliest tool makers is given by the skull of Pekin Man, with his shallow cranium, immense ridge jutting over the eyes and ape-like teeth. Yet to such brutish creatures is due the honour of conceiving the first deliberate artificial creation ever known on the planet Earth, or as far as we know in the universe. Never has originality been

8

MEGALITHIC TOMB AT PENTRE IFAN, PEMBROKESHIRE

Oil painting by Richard Tonge of Bath, 'painter and modeller of Megaliths,' c. 1830

STONEHENGE, WILTSHIRE

more fundamental than that shown in the battered pebbles that were their tools. Ape-men such as these certainly lived in the British region before the Ice Age, and Englishmen were outstanding among the pioneers who studied and saw the significance of their crudely chipped flints. We can picture them roaming our country in small family groups with no wider social organisation, killing such game as they could with their inefficient, unspecialised implements, but probably relying to a large extent on vegetable food or on grubs and other small creatures.

This, then, was the hesitant yet all-important beginning to his mysterious career which man had made before the beginning of the so-called Ice Age of Europe, that stretch of several hundreds of thousands of years during which intensely cold periods were divided by warmer ones. During the height of the glaciations the northern ice-sheets extended to cover most of Britain lying north of a line joining the Wash and the Bristol Channel. During the warmest intervals this country was tropical, there were hippopotamus in our now familiar valleys, elephant ranging our mild domestic hills.

Such climatic upheavals were a severe test for the European mammals and very many species succumbed. Man, cunning and adaptable, survived and developed under the stimulus of the ordeal. It was, indeed, the most crucial time of his biological history. At the beginning of the Ice Age hardly to be distinguished from others of the primates, by its end he looked very much like ourselves. Similarly, beginning the period equipped only with the most elementary of tools he ended it with a material culture equal to that of many surviving peoples.

It is probable that this development of our species was in part due to contrasts and conflicts such as we have to admit, however unwillingly, may still be a means for promoting growth and change. For it seems that in addition to the adaptability demanded by the climate, there was a further stimulus provided by the existence during the Ice Age of two main human types contrasting both in physique and in material culture. One of these was evolving towards modern *homo sapiens*, the other, physically far more ape-like, was in Europe to culminate and die out in the famous Neanderthal men. The first type, which had a mainly southern range across Africa and India, used as its most characteristic implement a large pear-shaped all-purpose tool like that on page 13. It is interesting to reflect that for such an immense span of history men in Britain and in India encountered their environments with an almost identical equipment. These hunters lived in Britain during the inter-glacial periods, their implements are common in gravels and other deposits in southern and eastern England, and fragments from the skull of one of them were recently found in one of the terraces laid down by the Thames. This Swanscombe man is now famous : it is an odd series of chances which, narrowing down through the millennia, singles out for preservation and discovery one individual for posthumous fame, a fame which falls also upon the locality where the bones have lain so that obscure English place-names like

Piltdown or Swanscombe are suddenly made familiar in world literature. The other and more simian men occupied a generally more easterly territory extending across Asia as far as Mongolia; their tools tended to be lighter, being made from flakes instead of lumps of flint or stone. We know from the presence of flake tools that Britain fell within their range, although human remains are as yet limited to a few of the characteristically massive Neanderthal teeth found in a Channel Island cave.

After remaining largely distinct from one another during the earlier part of the Ice Age these two stocks later began mutually to react; sometimes to borrow, sometimes perhaps to impose, cultural ideas upon one another. What this in fact meant in terms of primitive trade, of raids and savage battles we have to guess, but certainly one result was to stimulate far more rapid change. Brought face to face with other ways of doing things, timeless conservatism was broken down and men became more experimental, more observant.

The immediate outcome of this period of rivalry was the success of *homo sapiens*, its latest consequences, ourselves. The Neanderthal men died out and our own species began the sudden acceleration of its development which was within a measurable time to lead to civilisation and that urban life by which man came to live in a world of his own, walled off from the natural environment through which he had wandered since his earliest days.

During this first period of the full ascendency of *homo sapiens*, ending about 10,000 B.C. when the ice-sheets were year by year melting away to the north, western Europe enjoyed most favourable conditions. It was a period of natural economic abundance. On open steppes, which to us would still have seemed most disagreeably cold, lived herds of reindeer, bison, horse, and, in the earlier phases, mammoth. For game-hunters it was paradisiacal, and a paradise which they were now equipped to exploit. Spears and harpoons were skilfully and even beautifully shaped from stone and bone, while the invention of the spear-thrower made it possible to kill at a distance. So for the first time human societies were not entirely enslaved to the quest for food. They had time to do nothing and so to think of other things to do. Recent societies have made it a habit to devote a very large part of their surplus energy to the production of an endless multiplication of material goods, almost every individual among us owning hundreds or thousands of objects whose mere maintenance is a heavy tax. If this was already less true in the Middle Ages when much of the social surplus of time and labour was devoted to the church it was altogether otherwise in the period of European history we are considering. Certainly the later Old Stone Age hunters did improve their material culture, but a great part of their new leisure must have been given to ritual life, including a ritualistic art. A parallel was to be found until recently among the Indians of the north-west coasts of America who were equally fortunate in their control of an easy food supply. These tribes evolved an incredibly elaborate ritual life based on a hierarchic society in which symbols of vast wealth (the equivalent of a million pound bank draft to

MAP OF THE BRITISH ISLES SHOWING THE CHIEF PLACES MENTIONED IN THE TEXT

a modern magnate) were ceremonially destroyed by the chiefs as steps towards higher social and religious prestige. There can be no evidence of such customs among the Old Stone Age Europeans, but there are many surviving signs of other ceremonies. They had magicians who performed their dances dressed in the skins and horns of wild animals, and in one cave at least men had leapt on their heels round and round finely modelled clay images of bison; they carved voluptuous female idols as personifications of fertility and to secure good hunting they painted and engraved likenesses of the game animals in the deepest recesses of caves. Art flowed also on to objects of use, on to spear-throwers and other implements of bone or ivory. With perfect skill animal forms were adapted : the horns of an ibex curve back strongly round a shaft, the tail of a reindeer projects as a stop for the butt of a spear.

In short, while nature was benign, the romantic picture of the happy savage was, perhaps, not so far wide of the mark. Life must often have been short, but not unduly hard or monotonous.

In all this the British region had only an impoverished marginal share, being still too cold to support any considerable population.* Nevertheless, hunting families did from time to time occupy suitable caves such as those in Cheddar Gorge, in south Devon (Kent's Cavern), the Derbyshire ravines, Yorkshire, and even Scotland (Oban), and already before the end of the Old Stone Age they had developed a culture, though a poor one, which was characteristically their own. Before even it was isolated, therefore, the British region had begun to modify continental traditions, a process which was to continue throughout its history.

This native British culture belonged essentially to the Old Stone Age, but it was to last on into a new epoch, that of the Middle Stone Age. As average temperatures rose degree by degree through the centuries, forest encroached on steppe, trees rooted themselves where the game herds had enjoyed open grassland. The fauna of Europe was entirely changed and men had to adapt their habits to fit themselves into the forest landscape wherever there was room, along the edge of lakes and rivers, in sandy country and by the seashore. Game was smaller and more difficult to obtain and the diet had to be made up by the collection of shellfish.

It was during the Middle Stone Age that an event took place which still appeals to the imagination : the isolation of our country from the continent. It is tempting, though shockingly unwarranted, to think that there may have been one dramatic hour when it ceased to be possible to walk dry-foot from France to Britain. I like to imagine a stormy winter night when a wave overtopping the precursors which had prepared the way, smashed the last tenuous ridge of chalk somewhere between Kent and the Pas de Calais and swept over it to make Britain an island. In whatever way this event did in fact take place it would have been of little concern to the small population pre-occupied in wresting a living from its scattered and isolated hunting grounds.

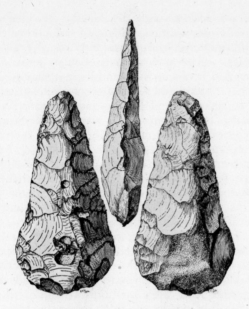

PALÆOLITHIC HAND-AXE
Dorset

FIRST FARMERS

HAD they been left to their own devices it is not impossible that the Middle Stone Age tribes might have continued their food-gathering economy indefinitely and remained as primitive as those of North America, Africa or the Pacific at the time of their discovery by Europeans. As it was, however, the turn of Britain to be settled by a people at a much higher stage of culture came some 4,500 years ago and by means not really analogous to the later European expansion. For whereas Columbus, Vasco da Gama or Cook and the colonists who followed them went as civilised individuals directly from their homelands to their various distant goals, the expansion of higher culture from the early centres of civilisation in Mesopotamia and Egypt took place only very gradually as traders groped their way towards new sources of wealth, and peasants pushed their fields ahead in their need for fresh soil. In the Near East farming communities were already established before the 5th millennium B.C., and advanced urban civilisation had followed in the Mesopotamian and Egyptian river valleys by 3000, but it was not until five centuries later that their influence was felt in Western Europe. This slow spread naturally meant lack of contact between the centres of high civilisation and the remote peripheries of their influence. How great the disparity can be is shown even now within the compass of a small country where we are familiar with the contrast between London and the still all but prehistoric communities of Western Ireland and the Scottish Isles.

Urban life, then, was already old in the East when, from about 2500 B.C., boatloads of farming colonists crossed to Britain from Northern France and the Low Countries to take possession of the upland system of Southern and Eastern England. Other colonist seafarers came more directly from the Mediterranean to occupy much of Ireland and spread right up our Atlantic seaboard as far even as the Orkneys. The newcomers brought in their boats cattle and sheep, seeds of wheat, and in their heads they brought hitherto unknown skills : weaving, potting, as well as the whole business of mixed farming. There was in the main areas of upland settlement a complete break with Middle Stone Age tradition ; the basis of the economy was now the breeding of stock, supported by corn-growing on a small scale ; hunting, although it was still practised, became surprisingly unimportant economically. With a good supply of domestic meat, wheat flour and dairy produce, together with the means for better cooking offered by the use of pottery, food must have been far nicer as well as far more nutritious than in the Middle Stone Age, which, in the imagination, reeks of shellfish. The wide horns and great bulk of the cattle suggest an admixture of the decorative wild species, *primigenius*, with the new shorthorn stock. They were pastured with the sheep, a small breed, on the hills, while the swine must have been given the run of the oak forests which everywhere flooded round the uplands like a sea. The small irregular corn plots, worked by the women with hoes or digging sticks, would have lain near the dwelling places. What is most difficult to discover is the basic fact of how far these earliest farming communities had fixed settlements, how far they made seasonal movements or frequent shifts to new cultivable ground. All along the southern hill country from Sussex to Devon they raised roughly circular earthworks with several concentric rings of banks and ditches interrupted at short intervals by gaps and causeways. These were ambitious undertakings, they mark, indeed, the first serious onslaught on the face of Britain made by man for domestic and social purposes, but how they were used we have not yet learnt. It is true that the ditches may contain the usual filthy litter of primitive occupation, bones, broken crocks, dead dogs and an occasional human corpse, but no trace of the huts of a regular village has ever been found inside the earthworks. It may be, therefore, that they were used only seasonally, perhaps when the herds had to be rounded up before the winter.

While these farmers of ultimately Mediterranean origin were occupying the hills there was also, particularly in the eastern part of the country, another element in the population of Britain largely made up of Middle Stone Age stock reinforced by immigrants from Scandinavia. These societies, often living in river valleys, seem still to have relied very considerably on hunting and food gathering and to have been generally more primitive than the upland peoples.

SILBURY HILL, NEAR AVEBURY, WILTSHIRE
Water colour by James Bridges, 1819-1853

Far the most vivid and intimate picture of a New Stone Age community is to be found remote in the Orkneys where the stone-built hut-cluster of Skara Brae has been preserved through thousands of years by drifting sand dunes. In absolute date this village belongs to the early Bronze Age of the south, but its inhabitants had no metal and followed a characteristically New Stone Age way of life. There were some half-dozen houses consisting of a comfortably sized room, measuring as much as 20 by 18 feet and with small side closets let into the walls. Furniture, all made from sheets of Caithness flagstone, included a shelved dresser, wall shelving, and beds warmly hung with skin canopies; a peat fire burned on a central hearth. The huts were linked by narrow alleys completely roofed in for protection against Orkney gales and were served by what appears to have been a communally owned workshop. Hygiene and barbarism are not often associated, but the Skara Brae villagers had laid under their houses not only an efficient sewerage system, but also the bodies of two old women, presumably a sacrifice. These people were pastoralists, and good pasture enabled them to remain as a settled community for generations, living in a state of completely isolated self-sufficiency now difficult to conceive. There they were in their little enclosed warren, perhaps some thirty to fifty of them, getting their clothing from the skins of their herds, food from their flesh and milk, eked out by shellfish from the

15

nearby shore; their houses, furniture and utensils they cut from the native rock. Communal self-sufficiency, though seen in its most dramatic form in this remote island, was characteristic of New Stone Age economy; while to-day we may be ruined by events on the continent of America, these farmers depended on little outside the bounds of their own pastures. There was, however, one exception to it on a scale large enough to be of some significance. The axe or adze was at this time an indispensable tool, serving to fell trees, for rough carpentry and also, no doubt, for use as a hoe. As it was comparatively large and demanded good material it could not well be made from surface pebbles. To meet this need a specialised industry grew up. In the highland country the most suitable rocks were quarried from the mountain side, as at Graig Llwyd, Penmaenmawr, shaped into axes, and very widely traded. In lowland England on the other hand the staple material was flint. Mining has come to have a very particular significance in British history; here was its beginning. To reach the big easily worked nodules of flint that lay bedded in the chalk, shafts were sunk, sometimes as deep as seventy feet, and a maze of galleries driven along the flint seams. The nodules, once hoisted to the surface, were worked up on the spot and the axes distributed over the greater part of the country. The most famous mines are those of Grimes Graves in Norfolk, but the rash of hollows and bumps that in chalk country marks their filled-up shafts can be seen in many places on the South Downs and more rarely in Wessex.

In their religious practice, more than anywhere else, the New Stone Age colonists showed their Mediterranean antecedents. It is most clearly evident in the tombs which form the outstanding religious architecture of the time. Among the various groups of seafarers who settled along the coasts of Western Britain, religious observances with the power and prestige which they gave were of great importance. They appear to have centred on the communal graves which these people at vast effort raised for their dead. They were built with chambers of great stone slabs, made cave-like and mysterious by enveloping mounds, sometimes of very great size. Here the dead were buried with elaborate ritual, while the entrances were often designed to provide the formal setting for religious ceremonies. Fine examples of such megalithic tombs, which fall into many differing architectural groups, are the Cotswold long-barrows with their attractive names—Hetty Pegler's Tump, Belas Knap, the Toots—huge chambered round cairns such as New Grange in Ireland, and a variety of imposing tombs along the Scottish coast and among the islands from Kintyre to the Orkneys. Those in Cornwall are well known and often impressive standing in that strange, ancient landscape, but most of them are architecturally poor and degenerate.

Among the population of the chalk hills of southern and eastern England, and the culturally related areas of the Lincolnshire and Yorkshire Wolds, the place of these megalithic monuments was in part taken by earthen long-barrows which originally often had chambers, façades and other architectural

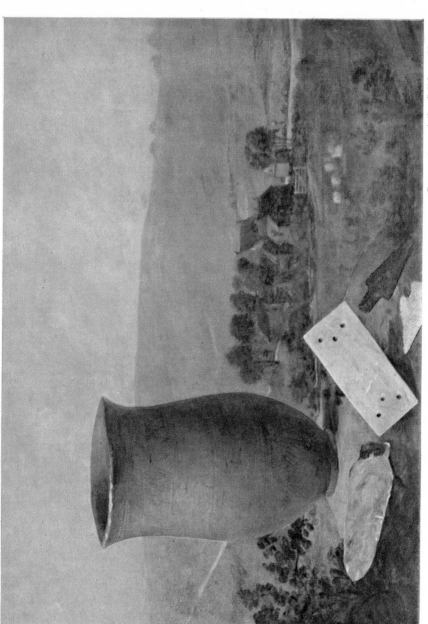

FINDS FROM A ROUND BARROW AT WINTERSLOW, WILTSHIRE

Bell beaker, two flint arrow-heads and a bracer to protect the wrist from the bow-string

Oil painting by Mr. Guest of Salisbury, 1814

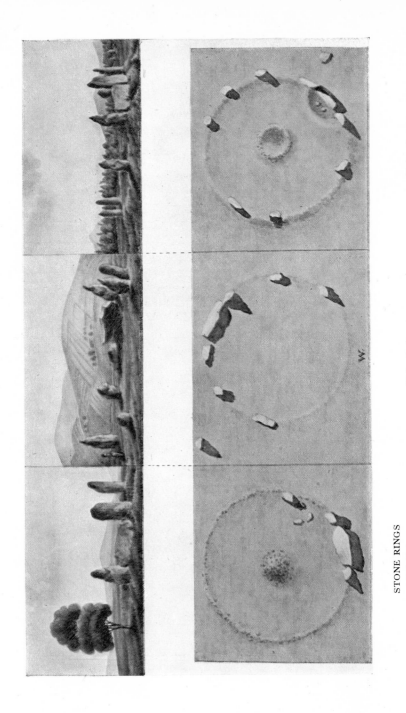

STONE RINGS

Old Keig

Balquhain

Balgorkar

Water colour by I. Logan, 1827

features in wood. These long-barrows, still such a familiar sight on our chalk hills, were used for communal burial, but, unlike the practice in megalithic tombs, the bodies must often have been interred all at one time.

British megalithic architecture, and to a lesser extent that of the long-barrows, owes its origins to the Mediterranean. In most of the secondary centres of civilisation, Iberia, the Balearics, Sardinia, Sicily, Malta, Crete, those stepping stones by which Near Eastern civilisation reached the West, there are tombs and other monuments which recall its characteristic features. Equally was this true of other elements of New Stone Age religion. Though both rude and rare, female statuettes of this time have been found in Britain, by far the most important being the seated figure found together with a carved phallus in one of the shafts of the Grimes Graves flint mines. The Earth Mother goddess is, of course, a well-known figure in the Mediterranean at this period and before; in art she is represented in many conventions, from the austere beauty of the Cycladic statuettes to the fearfully exaggerated obesity of the Maltese figures. There can be no doubt that these are reflections of the Mediterranean fertility religion and that they are directly connected with the megalithic cult of the dead. In France female symbols are carved on standing stones and megalithic tombs, a notable Breton example showing two pairs of round bosses carved in high relief to represent breasts. Britain has nothing so remarkable, nothing so unambiguous, to show anywhere; but the whole symbolism of megalithic architecture with its dark earth-fast chambers points towards a cult of fertility, the earth mother, death and rebirth. This is in strong contrast with a new symbolism, that of the male sky god soon to be introduced into Britain by the invaders of the Bronze Age. The one is here seen to be characteristic of peasant communities, probably originally matriarchal in their organisation; the other of strongly patriarchal nomadic pastoralists.

The New Stone Age lasted for over five hundred years. During that time there was firmly established in this country the farming economy which, despite constant modification, was to be the mainstay of our society until the Industrial Revolution. Its introduction not only revolutionised human life, but changed the appearance of Britain. For the first time man began to make an impression on the natural landscape. The early hunters threading the forests and driving game on the steppes can have made little more mark on their surroundings than the animals that shared them. But now Britain must have looked humanly inhabited. There were homesteads and settlements, however flimsy, with their cultivated plots; there were conspicuous entrenchments cutting the chalk; there were domestic herds not only noticeable in themselves, but helping also to keep vegetation in check and hill-tops open, and with their good stone axes men could even nibble away a little at the fringes of the forest. Finally in many regions this setting of material life was dominated by the great ritual monuments, just as cathedrals and churches were later to dominate our cities and villages.

THE PASTORALISTS

IT was probably among the later generations of the western megalith people that British metallurgy was first developed. Here was an enterprising people with close historical, and perhaps even personal, contacts with south-western Europe where metal was already in use, settled in just that region of Britain where copper and tin could most readily be found. Simple flat axe-blades cast in open moulds were early made from Irish copper, while when the knowledge of bronze became more general the tin necessary for the alloying was to hand in Cornwall. It was about 4,000 years ago that the first Irish smiths initiated an industry that was to take a notable part in the foundation of European civilisation.

Yet it was not these slight, dark Mediterraneans of the west who themselves provided the force needed to launch the Bronze Age in Britain as a whole. This came from the opposite direction when our east and south coasts were invaded by tribes who began sailing from France and the Low Countries in about 1800 B.C. These invaders, who have been known as Beaker Folk from their curious and distinctive drinking pots, had a warlike tradition; they were archers, some were armed with polished stone battle axes and they had an acquaintance also with the advantages of metal. Probably few of them actually brought metal equipment with them from the continent, but they were quick to exploit the work of the Irish smiths who supplied them with daggers, axes and other small objects in bronze. So it was the demand of these powerful conquerors that really established the use of bronze in Britain, rare and costly though it was, to remain for several centuries. Their demands were not only utilitarian : the Beaker Folk also liked to wear ornaments of Irish gold. The ore came mainly from the Wicklow hills and the Irish craftsmen worked it into sheets, shaped and chased it with some skill. During the rest of the Bronze Age, Irish gold was to be imported not only into Britain but into continental lands from Denmark to southern France, adding a fine lustre to barbarian Europe. The Beaker Folk overran England, Wales, and much of Scotland, though few reached Ireland, and wherever they penetrated strongly seem to have lorded it as a warrior aristocracy, dispossessing and enslaving the New Stone Age population. This must have been a time when the reality of racial contrasts was most forcefully shown. Though of mixed stock and containing round-headed Alpine elements, many of the Beaker Folk were descended from the northern warrior peoples and probably spoke an Indo-European language—some indeed now believe that it was they who introduced a speech from which Erse and Gaelic are descended. They would, therefore, have been strikingly unlike the Stone Age population of the uplands : taller, more heavily built and more heavily featured; in colouring generally much fairer. The big fair men dispossessing the small dark. These events in Britain were only the most westerly of many such clashes occurring at this time of migration in the centuries on either side of 2000 B.C.

GOLD LUNULA
Athlone, Co. Roscommon, Ireland

Throughout the whole of this country there are only two or three wretched hut-sites surviving as witness of any settled domestic life among the Beaker Folk. It is, indeed, likely that they were more nomadic than their predecessors, pastoralists with an even more exiguous agriculture, and living mainly in skin or felt tents or the flimsiest of huts.

It would be wrong to draw a crude contrast between an agricultural Stone Age peasantry and a conquering aristocracy of nomadic pastoralists, but there is some truth in the picture. It is to be expected that the Beaker Folk would show some of the traits of nomadic society so familiar among the early Indo-European-speaking peoples. Most significant among these traits is the tendency to a high patriarchal order of society by which the male head of the family group is absolute master not only of the herds and of the depressed classes of bondmen and enslaved races, but also of his own women and chil-

19

dren. Nevertheless, this domination accepted, the women were not ill placed. Their ability to share on equal terms in much of the pastoral work, and their importance as the bearers of the children, vital in a pastoral economy, gave them their own high value. A strong, fertile, skilful woman would exchange for many head of cattle and, therefore, had her status. Furthermore, women in nomadic society may expect less drudgery than peasant women because there is less temptation to accumulate exacting possessions, less cleaning, too, and because the preparation of meat and milk foods is easier than the grinding, baking and fuel-gathering demanded by a cereal diet.

Nowhere is a northern warrior-pastoral element in the Beaker culture more evident than in its religious practice. Most characteristic, instead of the communal burial of neolithic society, Beaker chiefs and their women were usually buried individually, each body under its own mound, a rite obviously in harmony not only with a necessity imposed by nomadism, but also with the patriarchal, individualistic outlook. So it was that they were buried, these lordly "shepherds of the people," in isolated state crouched on their sides and accompanied by their drinking vessels and the few weapons, tools and ornaments that then represented wealth. There they lay and were covered by the round barrows which were to remain such a well-known part of our landscape, and there lay until one by one they were discovered in historic times, first by puzzled peasants whose ploughs gradually bit down into their graves, then by antiquaries seeking a learned reputation or objects for their cabinets, and last by the mechanical excavators of factory and aerodrome, or by scientists hunting facts with all the paraphernalia of modern excavation.

Also characteristic were the religious temples now for the first time built in Britain. A comparison has already been made between the earth-mother cults of the Mediterranean peasants and the 'Indo-European' sky god. Without taking too seriously the more elaborate astronomical studies which have been made, we can see in Stonehenge, Avebury and the lesser monuments, centres for religious ritual directed towards the sun and the heavens. The most typical feature of these Beaker temples was the enclosing circular earthwork seen at its most imposing in the vast ring of Avebury, but also well shown in Maumbury Rings (adapted to make a Roman amphitheatre), Gorsey Bigbury on Mendip, Stennis in the Orkneys, and a number more throughout Britain. Within were more or less elaborate circular settings of large stones or wooden posts, sometimes, as at Arminghall in Norfolk, of entire tree trunks.

Stonehenge is unique in the careful shaping of all its stones, in the use of lintels held in place by mortice and tenon and in its horseshoe-shaped setting of huge trilithons. At least equally remarkable is the fact that the famous "bluestones" were carried two hundred miles from Pembrokeshire, where they had evidently formed part of some more ancient monument. The small central enclosure of Stonehenge, lying at the foot of the towering trilithons and with the recumbent altar slab at its inner end, must have been the most sacred area in Britain.

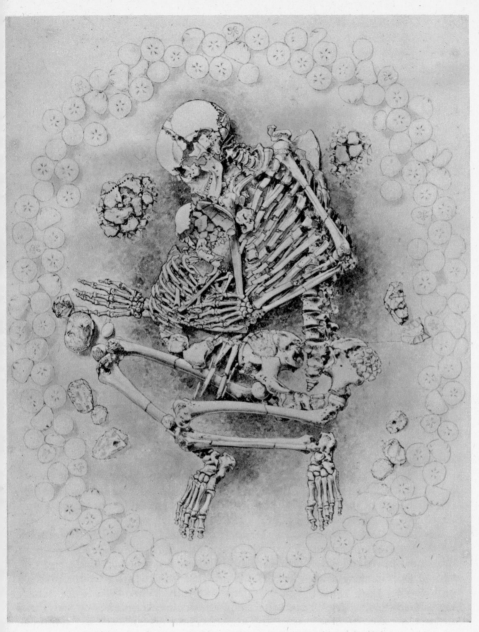

CROUCHED BURIAL IN ROUND TUMULUS ON DUNSTABLE DOWNS
Ink and wash drawing by Worthington G. Smith, 1887

21

MEGALITH IN CLATFORD BOTTOM, NEAR AVEBURY, WILTSHIRE
Water colour by James Bridges, 1819-1853

Avebury, with its massive sarsen stone rings, has little of the architectural sophistication of Stonehenge, but is impressive in its reckless size. The circular bank, which rises fifty feet above its own ditch-bottom, encloses nearly thirty acres and the stone circle set just inside is the largest in Europe.

It must have been a most compelling religious emotion which provoked the raising of these extraordinary sanctuaries by a people who had only stone mauls to shape masonry, antler picks and shoulder-blade shovels to dig banks.

Free-standing stone circles such as the Rollright circle are distinct and often belong to a later phase of the Bronze Age. Equally with the religious, the social implications of the Beaker temples point to a more mobile society made up of less rigidly self-contained communities. Not only must very many workers have been required to build them, but the commanding position of Stonehenge and Avebury at the centre of the English upland system suggests that they were Meccas designed to draw tribesmen from far off. One can imagine that at the time of the chief festivals the uplands were drained of half their population. From the North and South Downs, the Chilterns and East Anglian Heights, from the Cotswolds and Dorset hills, and sometimes even from the Yorkshire and Lincolnshire Wolds, they must have made their journeys to join in the ceremonies of Avebury and Stonehenge, pitching their tents round about on the open downland.

The exhaustion of the first energy of the Beaker invasion was likely to be followed, as the Norman Conquest was followed, by a period when the old and temporarily submerged population reasserted itself to produce a stable culture combining old and new. This process was not, however, complete when soon after, in about 1700 B.C., it was interrupted in Wessex and the south-west generally, by the arrival of more invaders, few in numbers, but again coming as a strong warrior aristocracy. Their continental origins suggest that they were more purely of the northern warrior stock than the Beaker Folk and their coming may in fact be regarded simply as a reinforcement of that element in the Beaker culture. They continued the same pastoral way of life and similar religious practices—probably adding very largely to the architectural magnificence of Stonehenge. They introduced greatly improved methods for the bronze industry and were able to support the nomadic characteristic of "pride of birth and breeding" by a trade in foreign luxuries. They not only secured large supplies of amber from the Baltic, but were able for the first time to import into Britain manufactures of a near-eastern civilisation—even if these were no more considerable than Egyptian faience beads. They also appear to have interchanged goods with the rich Mycenaeans of

STANDING STONE AT STRATHE NEAR BARVAS, ISLE OF LEWIS
Drawn and engraved by William Daniell, 1819

23

Greece, but whether these still barbaric chiefs, whose wealth came from flocks grazing English hills, ever met merchant travellers who could give them first-hand accounts of court life at Mycene, of the Egyptian nobility and their sacred Pharaohs, who shall say? They must at least have had some hazy awareness that there, to the south, were societies quite unlike their own and far more splendid.

Meanwhile, north of the Thames, the re-emergence of the older population had gone forward undisturbed by any foreign ruling class such as that which had asserted itself to the south. Basically, however, the population on both sides of the river was closely akin : a mixture of Stone Age with Beaker Peoples.

When in its turn the new Wessex ruling class began to submerge into the rest of the population it had given an impulse to the spread over all Britain and much of Ireland of a single unified culture. This culture, known as the Urn culture, which extended northward over the country after about 1500 B.C. was built up of the contributions brought by all the various peoples who had crossed to Britain during the past millennium together with survivals from the still earlier aborigines, in much the same way that Norman, Dane, Anglo-Saxon and the underlying prehistoric population were, during the 12th and 13th centuries A.D., to come together as mediaeval England. It is like putting many metals into a crucible and pouring out, not just a mixture, but a new alloy with its own properties.

The five hundred years following 1500 B.C., then, was the time of consolidation for a strong and prosperous British culture. The way of life seems to have been predominantly that of Indo-European pastoralism, but the Stone Age element may, to some extent, have revived the economic importance of hunting, while on the other hand corn was, of course, still grown, though in primitive fashion. But the margin of prosperity was provided by trade. The great tradition founded by the Irish gold and bronze smiths had grown through the centuries and now, with metal in better supply, was producing rich ornaments and excellent tools and weapons. The use of double moulds, cores, and other improvements enabled the craftsmen to turn out axes, spears and rapiers which show a long-established, untroubled sureness of line and form. In their use of gold the older fashion for working with thin sheets now gave way to more massive forms such as the magnificent spiral torques. A fine example is that from Grunty Fen, which came up from the fenland peat gleaming as seductively as it had when still in the smith's hands.

During these five hundred years the population slowly increased and by their end, although the great stretches of forest remained untouched, communities had settled many of the poorer tracts of the country for the first time. And this population had formed a British culture too stubbornly established ever to be entirely obliterated even by the most violent of later happenings.

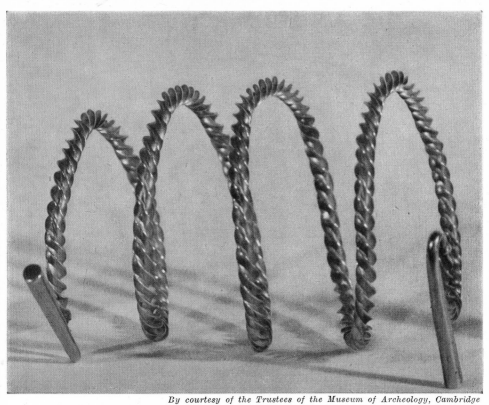

GOLD TORQUE FROM GRUNTY FEN, CAMBRIDGESHIRE

Middle Bronze Age

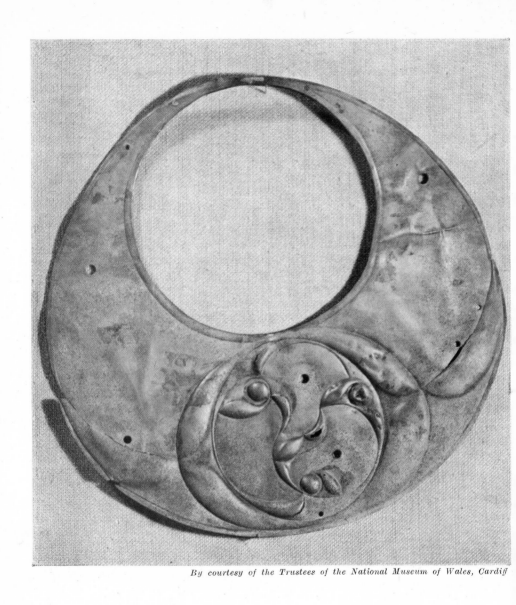

BRONZE CRESCENT FROM LLYN CERRIG, ANGLESEA
Example of La Tène Art

TO suggest that the middle phase of the Bronze Age was one of peace and neighbourliness would be absurd when, in fact, human invention had been bent to provide better weapons, while tools were largely neglected. But it is true that it was a period relatively free from external interference when Britain was left to build up its own distinctive culture. It was a respite which could not last when, towards the end of the second millennium B.C., Europe and the Near East were thrown into confusion by warrior migrations and wars : a troubled, heroic age whose strong colours have been made fast in Homeric literature. Repercussions, though remote, began to reach Britain after 1000 B.C. At first the changes were brought about largely by the infiltration of merchants and a few continental refugees, but soon there was a renewal of warlike invasions of tribes of Celtic stock, which were to continue intermittently up to the time of the Roman conquest.

Regarded heroically, the beginning of this period may be said to be marked by the appearance of that weapon so characteristic of the Indo-European warriors on the continent, the slashing sword. Regarded economically, it is distinguished rather by important developments in industry and food production which led to a larger and better equipped population.

The bronze industry was drastically changed and expanded. The metal itself was more plentiful, for copper by now may have been mined in Wales, northern England and Scotland, as well as in Ireland, and new designs and techniques were rapidly adopted. Smithies had become true workshops, specially planned and furnished. It is possible to reconstruct what is probably a sufficiently characteristic example. In a round hut with low stone walls the smith worked at a bench of stone slabs; for processes in which no great heat was required he could use the ordinary domestic fire that burnt in the middle of the floor, but for high temperature work he had a furnace built into the wall with blast provided by skin bellows. Nearby the furnace was the casting pit where the prepared mould was held upright in earth or sand ready for the pouring of the molten metal; there were also an upright slab to hold logs for the furnace and a flat stone for the pounding of ores, while there were recesses and shelves to take the smith's equipment of bronze, horn and stone hammers and the finer chasing and repoussé-work tools. For delicate gold work he might employ a diminutive instrument like a toy model of a modern blacksmith's anvil. Difficult techniques such as "casting on" made it possible to produce more elaborate shapes, while a most important development was in the hammering and riveting of sheet bronze. Sheet bronze was used for magnificent round shields and for cauldrons which, for the first time, made it possible to cook for large numbers at one time, cauldrons derived from Greek models of a kind familiar already in the Iliad, ". . . a charger yet untouched by flame; four ample measures held the shining frame."

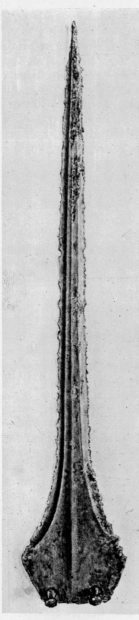

In the marketing of its goods the bronze industry was also revolutionised. Merchants travelled from steading to steading selling weapons, tools, ornaments and vessels new-polished from the bench, and buying up old broken articles to melt down as scrap. Probably these itinerants were a caste set apart from the settled communities which they served : free and unattached, like the gipsy tinkers of our own time, travelling sometimes overseas, they would have been held at once in awe and in scorn by the rest of society.

Certainly this reorganisation of the metal trade cheapened its products and so put them within the means of a wider section of the population. The expansion in absolute numbers of this population was made possible, and indeed inevitable, by equally drastic changes in agriculture, probably largely introduced by the Celtic immigrations which began in about 750 B.C. Since neolithic times there had been a decline rather than any progress in soil cultivation; it had remained a matter of small temporary plots which the women tilled by hand with hoes or weighted sticks. Now for the first time in the Bronze Age remains of settlements are frequent; southern and eastern England, the only regions directly settled by the newcomers, must soon have been scattered with permanent and more or less substantial farms surrounded by fields that were cultivated either with the foot plough, or a plough drawn by two oxen. The fields were still small—neat squarish fields very much like those still to be seen in south-western England and the west of Ireland. The ox plough, when it was used, had no coulter, no mould board for turning the sod, but simply a point to tear a furrow in the light upland soils which were still all that could be fully cultivated The ploughman probably went to and fro along the contours of the hillside, then up and down the slope over the same ground, like the crossing of a Victorian letter. It was an agriculture still simple and primitive enough, yet it so increased cereal food production

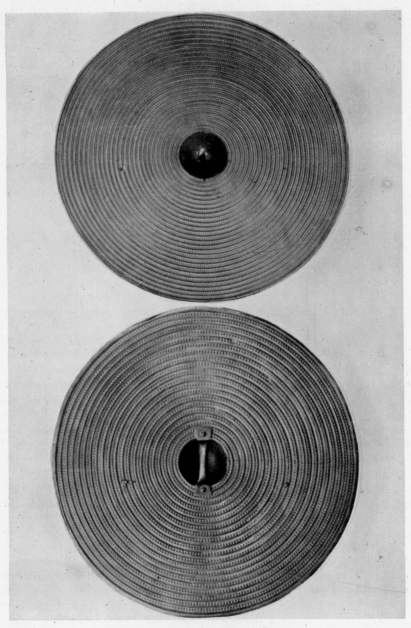

BACK AND FRONT OF BRONZE SHIELDS
Found at Moel Siabod, Caernarvonshire and at Rhyd-y-gors, Cardiganshire

27

GOLD GORGET, CO. CLARE
Original in the National Museum of Ireland, Dublin

that there was a rise in population sharper than anything known since the introduction of farming itself at the beginning of neolithic times. More corn, more
mouths. Herds remained no less important : indeed in at least some parts of
Wessex they were run on sizable ranches delimited and secured by long lines of
bank and ditch. Cattle now were all of the true Celtic shorthorn breed, the
ancient wide-horned *primigenius* strain having died out from the south of England.

The burial practice of the time clearly reflects a population larger and more
settled than before and possibly also more egalitarian. The dead were cre-
mated and buried in urns, either under round barrows or ranged many
together in big cemeteries, and they were left with few material signs of
pomp, with no lavish provision for the vicissitudes of another world. Indeed,
it is an age which has left little that is attractive or impressive. There are no
megalithic tombs to awe one with a massive gloom, no great temples survive
as the symbol of some magnificent conception, and military architecture is
almost equally lacking; there is no decorative art of any interest, no striking
new fashions in personal ornament; the bronzes, though some of the swords
are good, generally show a decline in form—the very cremation urns are
miserable in design and execution. Rather it was a time of technical advance,
of economic development.

In the Mediterranean iron was in full use by the beginning of the last millennium B.C., but it was some two centuries later that the earliest iron-using culture developed north of the Alps. This so-called Hallstatt culture, cradled in Central Europe, has obvious affinities with the contemporary pre-classical civilisation of Greece. It spread in time among the Celtic tribes of western Europe and, about 450 B.C., Celts crossing to Britain began the full introduction of the new metal. Its adoption there really only further developed the economic tendencies of the late Bronze Age : there is, in fact, an essential unity between the end of the Bronze and the beginning of the Iron Age. The new metal, whose ores were widespread and abundant and needed no alloying, made it possible to supply more and cheaper implements than a bronze industry could ever achieve. Its adoption, therefore, further improved the equipment of larger and larger sections of society. On the other hand, it did inevitably work a great change in gradually undermining the whole fabric of the bronze industry. No doubt some of the bronze-smiths adapted themselves and became blacksmiths, just as thirty years ago coachmen became chauffeurs, but they must have made the change equally grudgingly and with at least equally good reason, for much of its dignity would have left their trade. Not only was iron far less beautiful than bronze, there was no longer need to organise the supply of metal from distant sources, and, therefore, no need for wide commercial connections, no international market. Iron could often be obtained locally and the smith would be limited to working for his own community like any village blacksmith of recent times. There must, however, have been some comfort in the continued use of bronze for many ornamental purposes, while the most conservative of the bronze workers could continue their craft in the mountainous country of the west and north where iron was, for centuries, held at bay.

In their way of life as in industry the Hallstatt colonists generally developed late Bronze Age trends towards agricultural improvement and wider social

BROIGHTER GOLD TORQUE, COUNTY DERRY. LA TÈNE ART
Original in the National Museum, Dublin

29

organisation. The pattern of small fields round settlements must have spread out farther along the hillsides as the number of farms and hamlets grew. The farmsteads themselves were probably more elaborate. The main dwelling was still a round hut, but it might have a stout framework of wooden posts and a central clerestory to give light and ventilation. Outside in the yard, stoutly fenced or ditched, would stand small granaries for the seed corn, drying frames for the reaped ears, hollows where the grain could be winnowed and ovens where it could be dried for winter storage. Such winter storage was an important innovation, deep pits being sunk into the ground to hold the corn. It was a provision made necessary by the larger numbers which now had to be fed, and made possible by the substitution of settled homesteads for the nomads' tents. The size of settlements increased and small villages of clustering huts grew up, while many defensible hilltops were fortified first with palisades and ditches, later with much more formidable timber fronted ramparts. These strongholds may sometimes have been built merely as refuges for men and cattle in troubled times, but some were permanently occupied and they must certainly suggest larger and more developed social units, the first crystallising of the tribal organisation already strongly developed a few centuries later at the time of Caesar's invasion.

It is evident that in such conditions material standards of life would be raised and the domestic crafts thrive. Woven clothes must have been worn by most people and every well-established housewife would have her upright loom where she could make cloth that may, perhaps, have been enlivened by geometrical designs such as those that were traced on the pottery. Potting was still done at home for ordinary rough wares, but now special crockery, finer than anything known in the country before, was made commercially by experts. It was a pleasing ware, a warm glossy red decorated with grooves and incised designs, yet it seems very homely if it is remembered that when it was first introduced the potters of classical Greece were already producing their greatest masterpieces. Very soon Greek influence was to give Britain a school of art for which no apology need be made in any age or place.

CELTIC COIN FROM JERSEY
Back and front

BRONZE AND ENAMEL HORSE HARNESS. LA TÈNE ART
The Seven Sisters Hoard, Glamorgan

THE CELTIC ORDER

THE picture of the latest Bronze and earliest Iron Ages which irresist-
ibly takes shape in the mind is of an economically progressive society
without a highly privileged aristocratic class. Yet the mass of weapons,
the great swords and shields, the fortifications, must deny any simple conception of quiet peasant communities. The farmers could also be warriors,
and already tribal units were forming with their promise of perpetual warfare.
Nevertheless there may be truth in the idea that this was a period of relatively
equal society which was profoundly changed when, in the third and second
centuries B.C., parts of the country were conquered by arrogant war lords.
The situation may be likened to that of 1066. Saxon society had been
strongly stratified, yet it was clearly quite different from that which came into
being after the seizure of power by the Norman barons.

The fresh invaders were Celts, already possessing the La Tène culture
which had succeeded that of Hallstatt on the continent. It was a culture
begotten on the Hallstatt Celts by Greek and other southern influences which
reached them through their trade with the Mediterranean, in which slaves,
furs and various raw materials were bartered by the Celts for Mediterranean
products and particularly wine. Inevitably the Celts were influenced by
these contacts with civilisation and their craftsmen began to adapt to their own
taste the classical designs which they saw on imported luxury goods. Yet the
resulting La Tène culture, which first developed most brilliantly in eastern

31

France and south-west Germany, had somewhere in it also a strain of that strange, part oriental, genius of the Scyths.

Several La Tène groups reached Britain and took territory wherever they found it weakly held by their Hallstatt precursors. One wave came to eastern Scotland and spread right across to the Atlantic, another, as will be shown, reached south-western England, while minor footholds were won among the Hallstatt population in the south and east. Perhaps the most characteristic and important group were the warriors who conquered in Yorkshire and imposed their rule at least as forcibly as the Beaker Folk had done fifteen hundred years before. But now, at last, it is possible to fit an invading people with an historical and not an archaeological name. These were members of the Gaulish tribe of the Parisi, whose name the French have not allowed to die. As warriors they had a new strength for they introduced the use of the chariot, that spectacular instrument of war which Caesar's legionaries were to find so alarming. When the chiefs died, their chariots, rich harness, and sometimes their horses, were buried with them in graves more impressive than any that had been known in the country for many centuries.

The wealth of this new aristocracy was based on the usual Celtic economy of mixed farming from settled hamlets. It performed the first duty of an aristocracy in its support of artists, those crowning flowers on the economic body. For these Yorkshire Celts beyond all other groups seem to have been responsible for establishing the tradition of La Tène art which was to have so brilliant a future in this country. If anything can dispel the traditional picture of Britons as savages clad in woad and, for modesty's sake, hairy hearth-rugs, it should be the study of their art. The three centuries of its development, the various contributions made by distinct groups, can best be treated as a whole for its essential unity is far more striking than its superficial variety. It has survived almost entirely in metal work, with pottery and a few wooden objects as humble additions. It can only be guessed what has been lost of woven designs, leather, carving and embroidery. Nearly all the finest pieces are luxuries reflecting the taste of warriors who enjoyed personal magnificence and the trapping out of their wives and horses. Brooches to fasten the Celtic cloak, bracelets, necklaces, pins, hand-mirrors, harness fittings, bits and horse-armour, helmets, sword-scabbards and shields were among the chief vehicles of La Tène art. They show on the one hand strong plastic modelling, and on the other decorative design incised, in low relief, or picked out in coloured enamel. Both plastically and in the flat the Celtic work shows an extraordinary assurance, often a kind of wild delicacy, far surpassing its Greek prototypes, those stiff palmettes and other stylised botanical motifs. In the earliest continental pieces the Greek patterns are still recognisable, though from the first stretched, distorted and given life by the Celtic craftsmen; by the time the tradition was carried to Britain they were almost submerged in purely abstract linear forms. In these the finest artists achieved a marvellous control of balanced asymmetry in the design

THE DESBOROUGH MIRROR
Example of La Tène Art
Water colour by C. J. Prætorius

and equally in its related spaces. When, very occasionally, representational elements were used they were unnaturalistic, either fantastic like the horses on coins or on the hillside at Uffington, or more profoundly strange like the human masks on a bronze-bound bucket from Aylesford.

Perhaps it was about a century after the Parisi had first introduced their art in the north-east that other La Tène immigrants appeared in Cornwall and the south-west. Here the main purpose of conquest was probably commercial, to seize control of the Cornish tin trade which Pytheas had found thriving in the fourth century B.C. Indeed, these invaders may well have been kinsmen of the sea-faring Veneti of southern Brittany who, in Caesar's time, were controlling all the Atlantic coastal trade. In Cornwall itself they seem to have held the country from the round forts, such as Chun castle, which are so distinctive of this county; they also raised multiple ramparts across the neck of cliff promontories. Security of yet another kind was found by the Glastonbury and Meare marsh-dwellers within the palisades of the villages which they raised on artificial islands deep in the Somerset swamps. These settlements were probably made after the end of the second century B.C., and seem to represent a more easily established society and one in which prosperity had spread widely. At Skara Brae it was shifting sand which preserved a prehistoric village for posterity, here it was the bog. The peat was able to save not only the hard skeleton of their material culture, but some even of its soft parts : wood, wickerwork, basketry and cloth.

At its height the Glastonbury village must have had several hundred inhabitants living in some sixty round huts. These huts were usually over twenty feet across and had wattle walls and comfortable-looking conical thatched roofs. They do not appear to have been equipped with wooden furniture, perhaps this would have seemed too luxurious if the floor was still found serviceable for most of the acts of everyday life. Yet there were excellent carpenters in the village who could make carts and boats, tubs and ladles and even turn vessels on the lathe, there were also blacksmiths capable of supplying the village with all the iron implements it needed. Glastonbury pottery was of outstanding merit, the jars and bowls were sound in shape and decorated with Celtic patterns which are very pleasing, if not of the highest subtlety. There is always something moving in the continued use through scores of generations of the same simple things, and so at Glastonbury the strongest appeal lies in the dice-box, and in the bill-hooks with their curving tips, identical with those that trim our own autumn hedges.

The comfortable prosperity of this village came in part from commerce : Glastonbury has indeed been called an emporium. On the one hand it was linked by waterways with the Bristol Channel, on the other there was easy access to the Mendips and on into the whole of the southern uplands. There was certainly a trade in Cornish tin and Mendip lead, while bars of iron, probably from the Forest of Dean, served as a clumsy currency which was in circulation throughout the south-west and beyond.

During the day the Glastonbury settlement must have been active with small events; men and women going inland to attend their crops and herds, women at their domestic chores, hunters, fowlers and fishers setting off on their expeditions, craftsmen at work, dogs and children playing round the alleyways. But it is pleasant also to think of it in the evening when firelight showed through the doorways and smoke drifted into layers with the marsh mists. Perhaps it would be quiet in the village, while from beyond the palisade would come familiar sounds : the plop of a leaping fish, sharp cries of coots and sudden outbursts of excitement among the duck; swans, pelicans, bitterns and other heavy birds might rustle among the reed-beds and herons lift themselves leisurely into the air to fly inland for the night.

The marsh settlements, established some time after 100 B.C., were certainly occupied for over a century and for a time remained undisturbed by another invasion in the south-east that further complicated the already complex pattern of the later Celtic settlement of Britain. Late Bronze Age, Hallstatt, La Tène, all these incursions had left their mark on the still older population like waves impinging upon one another as the tide beats up a sandy slope. It seems to have been about 75 B.C. that another wave fell with the arrival in force in south-east England of Belgic tribesmen from the Low Countries. These Belgae were not wholly Celtic, but had a German strain in their ancestry, and it was this Teutonic part of their culture which made them important innovators when they reached Celtic Britain. They had a predominantly La Tène material culture and spoke a Celtic language, but it was the pattern of life characteristic of the great forest of Germany that was reproduced when they crossed the Channel and fitted themselves into the British landscape. Unlike the pure Celts they did not confine themselves to the hills, but often settled in river valleys or other open spaces in the forest. Excellently equipped with iron tools, they began to make some clearance of the hitherto almost untouched forests of this country to meet their agricultural needs. For the Belgae had begun to adopt a heavy wheeled plough, quite unlike the light Mediterranean form used by the other Celts. The new plough had a coulter and mould-board which could cut the sod and turn it over into those smooth, sloping ridges that are now so familiar. To draw this powerful instrument it might be necessary to yoke eight oxen, and to turn eight oxen round is an awkward and blasphemous business. So it was to lessen the number of such turns that some Belgic ploughmen made their fields very long and relatively narrow in strong contrast to the small squarish fields of the Celts.

This, then, was the greatest contribution of the Belgae. They took the first step towards the Middle Ages when they began to break down the ancient dependence on poor upland soils and to release the fertility of some of the heavier and lowland soils of Britain. These lands were no longer to nourish trees only, but men.

With this change in cultivation there inevitably went a shift in the siting of settlements : during the century before the Roman Conquest the Belgae did

MASK ON THE AYLESFORD BUCKET
La Tène art

much to move the tribal centres from fortified hill-tops to lower ground. Chichester was occupied in place of the Trundle, Winchester usurped the place of St. Catherine's Hill, and it was right on the banks of the Essex Colne that the ambitious Belgic prince, Cunobelin (Cymbeline), founded the first settlement in Britain which has some claim to be called a State capital. Cunobelin came to rule over the whole of south-eastern England, and his capital, Camulodunum, stood where now decaying fields await the spread of villas along the by-pass on the outskirts of Colchester. Behind long lines of rampart and ditch defending a wide area between two rivers was an untidy scatter of round and oval huts. Among them Cunobelin seems to have lived in a house only a little more substantial than the rest, though nearby he had his royal mint— a true coinage being another important Belgic innovation. Building was still barbarous at Camulodunum, but the manner of living must have been more civilised, for ships coming up the Colne unloaded at the wharf amphoræ full of wine, crates of fine Italian and Gaulish pottery and bronzes, with other goods brought in exchange for the corn, fatstock, metals, leather, slaves and hunting dogs which Britain could export to the Continent. Down by the wharf lived a commercial colony which could speak and even write some Latin : the inscriptions which they scratched on potsherds survive as the oldest handwriting in this country.

It was such traffic and cultural contacts with the Empire which helped to open the way for the Roman conquest.

Away from such securely protected centres as Colchester this last century of British independence showed all the turbulence to be expected of last phases. Britain was in a chaos of tribal warfare, and in particular the Belgic tribes were relentless in extending their conquests. Fortifications were raised by the Belgae, and against the Belgae, at a terrible expense of labour. This was the time when many of the famous hill-forts such as Maiden Castle and Hambledon Hill were raised to their greatest strength, their ramparts doubled and tripled. Step by step the Belgae pushed west and northward until, just before the Romans came to put an end to their triumphs, they destroyed the Somerset marsh villages. Perhaps it was they, too, who sacked Bredon Hill and set the heads of its defenders along their own gates.

Little has been said about Celtic religion ; when so much nonsense has been written about the Druids, reacting caution becomes almost excessive. Recently a find has been made which recalls that such bloody and warlike times had a cruel and bloody religion. Anglesea (Mona) was recorded by Tacitus as a great centre of druidism, and there, in a bog, was found a mass of Celtic treasures whose presence in such a remote region was, perhaps, due to a Druid community. Among the chariots, the harness, swords, spears and ornaments, which had probably been thrown as offerings into the bog, lay an iron slave-chain with five neck-rings. This, it has been suggested, was used to secure victims, probably prisoners of war, who had been selected for sacrifice.

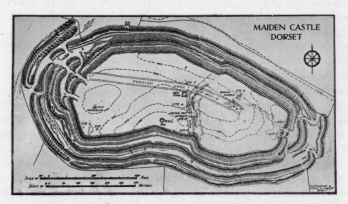

PLAN OF MAIDEN CASTLE, DORSET
From *Maiden Castle, Dorset* by R. E. M. Wheeler

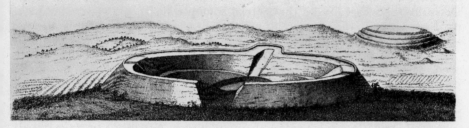

ROMAN BRITAIN
AND THE BARBARIAN CONQUEST

THE insane tribal feuds of the Celts did much to encourage the decision of the Emperor Claudius to order the invasion of Britain in A.D. 43. Nearly a century before this Caesar had been given a useful political opening for his British expeditions by the aggressions of the leading Belgic tribe of the Catuvellauni, and now again it was the actions of the Catuvellaunian royal house, and particularly the anti-Roman policy of Cunobelin's son, Caractacus, which gave Claudius the immediate pretext for an enterprise which had remained in the imperial mind since Caesar's premature essay. The defeat of Caractacus's army on the Medway, the carefully staged intervention of Claudius and his elephants and the prompt annexation of the great Catuvellaunian kingdom of south-east England are most familiar history. So also is the rapid conquest of the greater part of lowland England, but there is a recent discovery that reveals this campaign with all the power of a concrete detail to illumine a generalisation. On the left wing of the Roman advance, the IInd Legion, pushing south-westward, is known to have stormed a score of tribal hill-forts, among which Maiden Castle must have been included. Against the east entrance of that formidable fort were found the remains of the British defenders killed in the assault. The burials had been made in haste, and yet with traditional reverence, perhaps by the survivors creeping out in the darkness of the night after the battle. There lay the bodies of the defeated barbarians accompanied by vessels of their own native wares, but in the spinal column of one of them, token of the clash of two worlds, was lodged the iron head of a Roman catapult-arrow.

There followed the slow and dangerous campaigns to subdue the tribes of the western and northern hills. There was a generation of hard fighting and reverses in Wales and the north of England, and the appalling if heroic tragedy of the Boudiccan revolt before, towards the end of the eighties, the Romans had taken as much of Britain as was ever to be theirs. Still to the

37

FIGURE OF DIANA
Roman altar, London

north, in the Scottish highlands, the unconquered tribes remained in independence and prehistoric obscurity, some with an all but Bronze Age culture. Ireland stood apart, hardly to be reached even by the influence of trade.

The presence of these free and daring tribesmen made it necessary for the province of Britain to be very heavily garrisoned; throughout much of the occupation legions and auxiliaries numbered some 50,000 men, with legionary headquarters at Caerleon, Chester and York. The great northern wall built by Hadrian, still so impressive where it rides the north-country hills, symbolises a limit set to Roman power.

But away from the military areas of the west and north, Britain, before the end of the first century, was a subject and peaceful province. What were the effects of Roman conquest on the former prehistoric pattern of Britain? First, on the population. At any one time there may have been rather over 100,000 foreigners in the country, soldiers, merchants and officials, but most of these were in the military zones and the vast bulk of the population, perhaps about a million people, was descended from the old prehistoric stocks which we have seen gradually accumulating in these islands. From this accumulation the Roman Britons emerge as a very homogeneous stock, belonging unambiguously to the Nordic population which at that time occupied all north-western Europe.

Physically, then, the impact of Rome was slight. In social and material things it was naturally very great. Perhaps, most of us would think first of the roads, for have we not always been convinced, even in our perambulators, that when a dead straight stretch of road was before us it ran on Roman foundations? Certainly the road system that radiated from the hub of London was an essential part of Rome's mastery. It meant that for the first time the greater part of Britain was bound into an organic whole : that an idea forming in some authoritative mind in London had a reasonable chance of execution in Wales or along the Wall. But it was designed mainly for military needs and showed a martial disregard for the convenience of civilians, who must have relied largely on prehistoric tracks and ridgeways or built lesser roads for themselves.

The second great feature of Roman Britain which comes to mind are the towns—reminders of them are frequent both in material remains and in our place-names. Indeed, of late, since high explosive has disintegrated so much of the modern and mediaeval fabric of our cities, far more Roman work has been made visible, or at least accessible. Town life was essentially untried in pre-Roman Britain, for it has been said, with truth, that the Belgic settlements, even Camulodunum, were not cities but slums. Now all over the country new towns were planned with a methodical thoroughness never since equalled. No town-planner's dream could be more perfectly orderly than the Roman achievement. There was a regular gridwork of streets centred on a forum with shops and town hall, there was the amphitheatre for the entertainment of the citizens, the public bath-house for their health and social relaxation; water supply and drainage were efficient. There was munificence of public accommodation unheard of to-day: the colonnaded basilica or town hall and the amphitheatre could each normally accommodate all the inhabitants of a town with room to spare.

Most houses were modest buildings, long and narrow, often with a work-room opening on to the street, but others were more handsome with many large rooms, tessellated, frescoed and centrally heated. The houses were

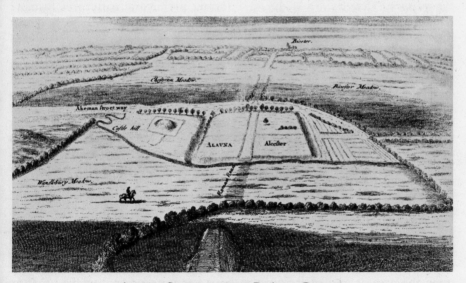

AKEMAN STREET AND THE ROAD TO BICESTER
Engraving by E. Kirkall after Stukeley

seldom crowded, sometimes, in fact, there was more open space than the Roman architects had intended, for not all towns grew to the extent which had been planned for them.

In the first and second centuries it was deliberate imperial policy to encourage the growth of towns in the new Province of Britain. The motive was, of course, mainly political : the towns were centres of local government whence Roman culture and habits would radiate to subdue unruly Celtic passions. But also many officials, brought up in the Graeco-Roman conviction that urban life was the highest form of human existence, must genuinely have felt that in towns they were offering the Britons their only escape from the slough of barbarism.

The status and function of the cities were naturally various. At first, to flatter native tradition, Colchester seems to have been the recognised capital of the Province, there the procurator lived, and the national assembly met to celebrate the obligatory imperial rites at the temple of the Divine Claudius. Later, perhaps even quite soon after the Boudiccan revolt, the irresistible economic attraction of London drew the centre of government to itself. While the civic status of London is unknown, St. Albans, where the Roman town of Verulamium was built near the old Belgic settlement at Prae Wood, was apparently made a *municipium*. *Coloniae*, that is citizen plantations of retired soldiers, were at Colchester, Gloucester, Lincoln and York—York, too, had special importance as a military headquarters.

The remaining, generally humbler, towns are in a way more interesting. Canterbury, Chichester, Winchester, Silchester, Cirencester, Dorchester, Exeter, Leicester, Wroxeter, Caerwent, Caistor-by-Norwich and Aldborough were tribal capitals, deliberately founded to divert old tribal loyalties into local government within the imperial framework. In the third century a change in official policy, together with the chaos of the Roman government caused a decay in towns throughout the Empire. They had been privileged, now they were over-burdened; and in Britain where the Celtic habit of aristocratic country life readily revived, the upper class, who had provided much of the wealth and government of the towns, retired to their estates where they could live very well on their own resources. Later official attempts to restore the towns failed, and in many of them the remaining inhabitants lived among decay : public buildings fell into the streets and the traffic merely went on over the wreckage; in what had been fine houses families camped in squalor, lighting their fires on the tessellated pavements : barbarians in the decline of a civilisation.

In the country it was quite otherwise. There was a general growth of prosperity throughout the Roman period which was only encouraged by the withdrawal of the wealthier classes from the towns. It must not, however, be forgotten that the country was then as much divided into two worlds as it has ever been : country life for the rich was quite unlike country life for the poor.

ROMAN MOSAIC PAVEMENT AT ALDBOROUGH (ISURIUM BRIGANTUM)
Coloured lithograph by J. E. Worrall, c. 1867

There was on the one hand the villa or country house, on the other the peasant village. But the system did not at all resemble that now surviving tenuously from mediæval times in which the landlord in his castle or manor dominates his tenants in the village. Instead the rich man's villa was a unit in itself; he, his family, and their household slaves occupied the house itself, the farm hands had quarters across the yard; all round stretched the fields of his estate.

The villages were equally independent and bore no relation to the villas; indeed, in regions such as Salisbury Plain and Cranborne Chase where such settlements are common villas hardly occur, and it may be that these

ROMAN VILLA AT NORTH LEIGH, OXFORDSHIRE, WITH FRAGMENTS FOUND THERE
Wash drawing by James Bridges, 1819-1853

areas formed imperial domains with the villagers as tenants of the State. Naturally the villas were centres of romanisation; their wealthy Celtic owners would not be without the orthodox Roman amenities, central heating, mosaic floors, fashionably painted walls, fine table services, bronze ware and linen. The peasant settlements, on the other hand, were little changed from pre-historic times—formless clusters of round huts. Rarely the most prosperous among them might have rather pathetic renderings of decorated plaster. It seems that even the agricultural methods differed, for while the estate owners probably often used the heavy plough and the open-strip field system first introduced by the Belgae, the peasants appear generally to have kept to the older Celtic light plough and small square fields.

Agriculture was, of course, by far the largest industry of Roman Britain, but the Conquest did much to stimulate others. As might be expected, in the first enthusiasm of romanisation there was a great demand for imported goods from the Empire, money was recklessly spent and money-lenders prospered, but soon home manufacture grew and supplied the needs of the Province. By the fourth century even wine was being produced at home. Exports probably remained much the same as those of pre-conquest trade, though it is doubtful if wheat could any longer be spared and the supply of slaves must have slackened with the ending of tribal warfare. British hunting dogs certainly were still widely popular, and other agreeable island specialities were oysters and their pearls.

The effect of romanisation, then, on the social and economic life of Britain was considerable. At the basis of it all, agriculture was not greatly altered, but industries were strengthened and multiplied and over all was imposed an entirely new system of communications, of towns and, on the frontiers, of military organisation. What was the effect on the other quite different things which men carry, often in the obscurity of unconsciousness, inside them-selves? There is a most interesting contrast between the reactions of native religion and native art. It is true that in the religious field druidism was eradicated as a cult dangerous to the State, but this cult had never been inseparable from the intimate gods of the people. The main Celtic pantheon, together with those lesser gods and goddesses that had their local habitation in groves and springs, united in perfect amity with the Roman deities. The Celts were willing to pay lip service to the official cult of the Divine Emperor and to identify many members of the classical pantheon with their own, while officials, legionaries and other settlers saw no impropriety in dedicating altars and in other ways showing respect to the native gods. The emotions that provoke the simpler religious manifestations are largely common to mankind; Roman and native found that they needed religious support to

ANGLO-SAXON BEADS
Drawn and engraved by F. W. Fairholt

43

URN OR CASTOR WARE FOUND IN THE SANDPITS AT BLACKHEATH
Water colour by Samuel Stanesby

meet much the same fears and desires, a spiritual symbolism for the same
simple human experiences.

It was not so with the expression of the æsthetic emotion. This is a thing
incredibly delicate in its poise; just as certain plants can flourish only on soils
with a highly specialised chemical composition, an artist is dependent on a
finely balanced soil of social structure, national temper, technical opportunity
and gradually accumulated cultural tradition. Even if the men who produced
the finest masterpieces of Celtic art did not call themselves artists and would
have been puzzled to know what was meant by the term, they were none the
less dependent on this fragile inheritance. When, therefore, upon their fine-
drawn, aristocratic tradition of non-representational art there descended with
absolute authority an already debased and bludgeoning tradition for natural-
istic representation, there could be no compromise. Celtic art was submerged

44

and the British craftsmen remained exceptionally inept in their spiritless attempt to imitate Roman models; the best that most of them could achieve was a droll clumsiness. It was inevitable in the circumstances. Consider what would happen if the most advanced in years of our Royal Academicians were suddenly put in complete control of the most advanced in views of our contemporary abstract artists. Indeed, perhaps adaptation was even more impossible for the Celts, for their abstract forms were more emotional and less intellectual than those of the present.

Yet throughout the Roman age there are signs that below the flood of provincial art something of the Celtic feeling survived; elusive yet unmistakable some unclassical spirit shows itself in a mosaic, a stone carving, a stray bronze ornament, or in the decoration of a Castor ware pot. It amounts to very little materially, yet is enough to make it not utterly surprising that after the Roman collapse native designers could re-emerge, even among the upheaval of the Anglo-Saxon invasions, to produce unmistakably British objects. This does not, of course, imply the active continuity of La Tène art through four centuries, but a persistent feeling for an abstract æsthetic expression utterly opposed to all classical ideals.

The period which saw the destruction of Roman Britain and the birth of Anglo-Saxon England is well known to be the most baffling in our history. From the historian's point of view there is no doubt of the obscurity of this Dark Age. Already in the third century cross-channel raiding by Saxon pirates necessitated the building of coastal forts such as Brancaster, Richborough and Pevensey and in the next century raids from Ireland and Scotland were menacing the Province on its other flanks. When in about 410 Rome at last withdrew all support, the unfortunate romanised provincials, now the unwilling receivers of independence, had to carry on as best they might. With

ANGLO-SAXON URNS FULL OF BURNT BONES FOUND NEAR ELMHAM, NORFOLK
Water colour by R. Elwes

45

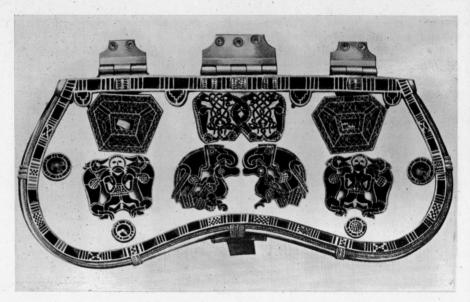

PURSE MOUNT OF GOLD AND JEWELS
From the Anglo-Saxon Ship Burial at Sutton Hoo

the old civil power removed, the Christian church, which had been growing in strength since the third century, became the best organised authority. But little could be done : at the most some attempt at local administration was maintained in the ruined cities, always threatened by attack from roving bands. After the last pathetic appeal for Roman help had been refused in 446, the Anglo-Saxon settlement began in earnest, no longer mere pillaging, but the steady occupation of British land. The invaders coming in along our southern and eastern coasts were pushing across the country, either absorbing and enslaving the British population or cutting them into isolated pockets. One great resurgence there was among the Britons surviving in the west; Ambrosius and Arthur (today reinstated as historical figures, the last of the Roman Britons), so vigorously defeated the Teutonic invaders that their progress was checked for decades. But in the end it was irresistible and Roman Britain was overwhelmed. Towns were destroyed, the villa system was completely broken and the Christian church obliterated. Only in east Kent were conditions rather different. Canterbury and other towns were never quite dead and there was some tenuous continuity between Roman and Anglo-Saxon institutions. There seems also to have been some survival in cultural tradition for a Roman element is visible in the magnificent Kentish jewellery blazing with gold and garnets and so unlike the uncouth, if effective, brooches and beads fashionable among the settlers in other areas. It shows equally, though less attractively, in the survival in Kent of wheel-made pottery which everywhere else gave way to hand-made wares.

To surviving Britons who clung to memories of imperial civilisation the triumph of the barbarians must have seemed a final, irreversible catastrophe, the end of all values. Yet the tough Anglo-Saxon farmers who cleared the forests and released for cultivation more and more of our best soils were preparing for a fresh uprush of civilised life quite different from that of Roman Britain, but ultimately so much stronger and more full of vitality. Everywhere settlements were being founded that were to take a place in Doomsday Book and grow into our own familiar villages and towns. How many of the English place-names that are so close a part of their countryside perpetuate the name of an adventurer of those times who, having seized his piece of land, cut the trees and built his farmstead, settled down to beget his contribution to the Anglo-Saxon nation?

A DEVON SIGNPOST

Feniton and Tallaton, Honiton and Whimple—
Still the endless stream of tongues,
Mothers', daughters', fathers', sons',
Chafe and smooth the syllables
As a river rounds its pebbles.
There the patient houses grow
While through their rooms the flesh must flow,
Mothers', daughters', fathers', sons',
On and on the river runs.
John makes way for younger John
But still the seasons stalk along,
Still the farm knows at its back
The comfort of the snug haystack.
Does the church tower bow its head
Because its bells must toll the dead?
Is it hateful to the furrow
That other hands may plough to-morrow?
Though sharp with curses, curved with songs
No agony of single tongues
Can dint the time-worn syllables
Smooth and round as river pebbles—
Feniton and Tallaton, Honiton and Whimple.

MAIN PERIODS
OF CIVILISATION IN BRITAIN

PALÆOLITHIC PERIOD	beginning c. 500000 B.C.
MESOLITHIC PERIOD	,, c. 10000 B.C.
ISOLATION OF BRITAIN	c. 6000 B.C.
NEOLITHIC PERIOD	beginning c. 2500 B.C.
BRONZE AGE	,, c. 1800 B.C.
IRON AGE	,, c. 500 B.C.
ROMAN CONQUEST	,, 43 A.D.
WITHDRAWAL OF ROMAN GOVERNMENT	410 A.D.

ANGLO-SAXON SETTLEMENT
{
Arrival of Hengist .. ..   443 A.D.
Battle of Mount Badon .. .. ..   c. 497 A.D.
St. Augustine's Mission .. .. ..   597 A.D.
}

A SHORT BIBLIOGRAPHY

Man Makes Himself by V. Gordon Childe, Watts 1936; Thinkers' Library 1939.—*What Happened in History* by V. Gordon Childe, Pelican Books 1942.—*Prehistoric Foundations of Europe* by C. F. C. Hawkes, Methuen 1940.—*The Personality of Britain* by Sir Cyril Fox, National Museum of Wales, 4th Edition 1943.—*Prehistoric Communities of the British Isles* by V. Gordon Childe, Chambers 1940.—*Prehistoric Britain* by J. and C. Hawkes, Pelican Books 1943.—*Prehistoric England* by J. G. D. Clark, Batsford 1940.—*The Prehistory of Scotland* by V. Gordon Childe, Kegan Paul 1935.—*Roman Britain* by R. G. Collingwood, Clarendon Press 1934.—*Roman Britain and the English Settlements* by R. G. Collingwood and J. N. L. Myres, Clarendon Press, 2nd Edition 1936.—*Celtic Ornament* by E. T. Leeds, Clarendon Press 1933.—*Anglo-Saxon Art to A.D.* 900 by T. D. Kendrick, Methuen 1938

MAPS: *Megalithic Survey:—Neolithic Wessex, The Trent Basin, South Wales;* Ordnance Survey. *Roman Britain;* Ordnance Survey